52

AWARD-WINNING
— TITLES —

EVERY **BOOK LOVER**
SHOULD READ

A ONE-YEAR JOURNAL

and Recommended Reading List from

the American Library Association

ALAAmericanLibraryAssociation

sourcebooks

The reviews in this book come from *Booklist*. *Booklist* is the book review magazine of the American Library Association and is a vibrant source of reading recommendations for all readers. It's been considered an essential collection development and readers' advisory tool by thousands of librarians for more than 100 years. For more information, visit booklistonline.com. To read *The Booklist Reader*, *Booklist*'s blog for book lovers, visit booklistreader.com.

Published by Sourcebooks
P.O. Box 4410, Naperville, Illinois 60567-4410
(630) 961-3900
sourcebooks.com

Printed and bound in the United States of America.
VP 10 9 8 7 6 5 4 3 2 1

CONTENTS

INTRODUCTION

Welcome, dear reader!

You are about to experience the crème de la crème of books published in recent years. This one-year reading journey invites you to explore a full listing of award-winning titles selected by the American Library Association.

The goal is not just to complete each title but also to relish the journey. Here's what you can expect: each week, you will be introduced to an award-winning title to read and cross off your list. A short write-up and review from the ALA will whet your appetite for the work, and a writing prompt is paired with each title so you can explore your thoughts as you read. The selected titles span genres and award categories, from Caldecott to Carnegie Medal winners!

With fun extras throughout, including additional book trackers for each season, this journal is a book club in your hands...and a reading adventure to savor.

Are you ready to read?

ABOUT THE AWARDS

Each year the American Library Association (ALA) honors outstanding books with awards and honors including the prestigious Andrew Carnegie Medal for Excellence in Fiction and Nonfiction, the Michael L. Printz Award for Excellence in Young Adult Literature, and the John Newbery Medal for the most distinguished contribution to American literature for children.

ANDREW CARNEGIE MEDALS FOR EXCELLENCE

The Andrew Carnegie Medals for Excellence in Fiction and Nonfiction, established in 2012, recognize the best fiction and nonfiction books for adult readers published in the United States in the previous year and serve as a guide to help adults select quality reading material. They are the first single-book awards for adult books given by the American Library Association and reflect the expert judgment and insight of library professionals who work closely with adult readers.

THE MICHAEL L. PRINTZ AWARD FOR EXCELLENCE IN YOUNG ADULT LITERATURE

The Michael L. Printz Award annually honors the best book written for teens, based entirely on its literary merit. In addition, the Printz Committee names up to four honor books, which also represent the best writing in young adult literature.

THE JOHN NEWBERY MEDAL

The John Newbery Medal, frequently shortened to the Newbery, is awarded annually by the Association for Library Service to Children, a division of the American Library Association, to the author of the most distinguished contribution to American literature for children. The Newbery is considered one of the most prestigious awards for children's literature in the United States.

MY ALL-TIME FAVORITE BOOKS

A place to track everything else I'm reading

READING LOG

Titles completed and everything else I am reading

DATE STARTED	TITLE	DATE COMPLETED

DATE STARTED	TITLE	DATE COMPLETED

The Poet X

ELIZABETH ACEVEDO

*Michael L. Printz Award for Excellence in
Young Adult Literature, 2019 Winner*

Xiomara is a little too much: a little too bold, too big, too much herself for her mother's taste. And sometimes, her big thoughts and feelings even overwhelm Xiomara herself. At times like this, her hardback notebook, a gift from her twin brother, is the crucible that turns her ideas and emotions into poetry. Through creating—and later sharing—this poetry, she begins to understand her relationships, claim her desires, and find her voice as a New York–Dominican girl and as a poet.

How do you speak up in your own life?

Lost Memory of Skin

RUSSELL BANKS

Andrew Carnegie Medal for Excellence in Fiction, 2012 Finalist

An unloved runt of twenty-two, the Kid thinks he might be "slightly retarded." With only a pet iguana for a friend, the Kid became addicted to online pornography, which leads to his becoming a virginal convicted sex offender on parole, camping out beneath a causeway at the water's edge in a city much like Miami. The Kid joins a veritable leper colony of sex offenders rendered homeless due to a law forbidding them to live within 2,500 feet of any place children may gather. Enter the Professor, a sociologist whose gargantuan mental powers are matched by his astonishing bulk. Humongous, arrogant, generous, brash, and secretive, the Professor, a character of startling and magnetic originality, latches on to the Kid first as a case study, then as an ally, until things go catastrophically wrong.

Who are the allies in your life?

----

52 Award-Winning Titles Every Book Lover Should Read

The Girl Who Drank the Moon

KELLY BARNHILL

John Newbery Medal, 2017 Winner

Every year, the elders of the Protectorate sacrifice a baby to appease an evil witch—though, in truth, it is a facade to subdue the populace. Xan, the witch in question, actually rescues each baby and finds families for them. One time, however, Xan accidentally feeds moonlight to the baby, which fills her with magic. Xan thereupon adopts her, names her Luna, and raises her with the help of a swamp monster and a tiny dragon. Luna's magic grows exponentially and causes such havoc that Xan casts a spell to suppress it until Luna turns thirteen. But the spell misfires, clouding Luna's mind whenever magic is mentioned, making proper training impossible. As the fateful birthday approaches, Xan fears dying before she can teach Luna everything she needs to know. Meanwhile, in the Protectorate, a young couple dares to challenge the status quo, a madwoman trapped in a tower escapes by way of paper birds, and a truly evil witch is revealed.

List your favorite fictional witches (good or evil) of all time.

The Line Becomes a River: Dispatches from the Border

FRANCISCO CANTÚ

Carnegie Medal for Excellence in Nonfiction, 2019 Finalist

Against his mother's advice, Cantú went to work for the U.S. Border Patrol in 2008; this memoir follows his work and its accompanying years-long struggle between darkness and light. He signs on in order to help people arrested for crossing the border ("I can offer them some small comfort by speaking with them in their own language, by talking to them with knowledge of their country"), and he describes his experiences patrolling a sector of the Arizona border where fearful and desperate migrants arrived dehydrated, crazed, and barely alive. Along the way Cantú is promoted twice, eventually tracking the individual movements of criminal organizations. Cantú offers explanations of the policies and realities that keep the border an intensely scrutinized topic of public discussion.

What compels you to read memoirs?

Moonglow

MICHAEL CHABON

Andrew Carnegie Medal for Excellence in Fiction, 2017 Finalist

"O, swear not by the moon, the inconstant moon," Juliet tells Romeo. Likewise, in this fictional biography, a young writer (who shares the author's name) knows not to accept as immutable his dying grandfather's tales. As he's listening to the final, unabridged versions of family stories, the writer's genetic and narrative legacy unfold. He learns about the woman his Jewish émigré grandmother was before madness overtook her; why his grandfather was so obsessed with rocketry and Wernher von Braun, and why he went to prison for attacking his boss with a telephone cord; and how an imaginary python led to a retirement-age romance.

What are the important stories of your family's history?

DATE STARTED:

DATE FINISHED:

MY RATING:

☆ ☆ ☆ ☆ ☆

Moonglow

The Water Dancer

TA-NEHISI COATES

Andrew Carnegie Medal for Excellence in Fiction, 2020 Finalist

Hiram Walker is the son of an enslaved woman and her slave master, owner of a prominent Virginia estate. When Hiram is nearly killed in a drowning accident, he detects an amazing gift he cannot understand or harness. He travels between worlds, gone but not gone, and sees his mother, Rose, who was sold away when he was a child. Despite this astonishing vision, he cannot remember much about Rose. His power and his memory are major forces that propel Hiram into an adulthood filled with the hypocrisy of slavery, including the requisite playacting that flavors a stew of complex relationships. Struggling with his own longing for freedom, Hiram finds his affiliations tested with Thena, the taciturn old woman who took him in as a child; Sophia, a young woman fighting against her fate on the plantation; and Hiram's father, who obliquely acknowledges him as a son. Throughout his courageous journey north and participation in the underground battle for liberation, Hiram struggles to match his gift with his mission.

How do you match your gifts with your mission?

52 Award-Winning Titles Every Book Lover Should Read

New Kid

JERRY CRAFT, ILLUSTRATED BY THE AUTHOR

John Newbery Medal, 2020 Winner

Jordan is anxious about starting seventh grade at an upscale private school where he is one of only a few kids of color. Those concerns are indeed merited, as Jordan confronts both covert and overt racism on a daily basis, casual assumptions about Black students' families and financial status, Black students being mistaken for one another, well-intentioned teachers awkwardly stumbling over language, and competition over skin tones among the Black students themselves. Yet it's clear that everyone has a burden to bear, from the weird girl to the blond boy who lives in a mansion, and, indeed, Jordan only learns to navigate his new world by not falling back on his own assumptions.

Has anyone ever made assumptions about you that were mistaken?

☆ ☆ ☆ ☆ ☆

Claire of the Sea Light

EDWIDGE DANTICAT

Andrew Carnegie Medal for Excellence in Fiction, 2014 Finalist

Seven-year-old Claire Faustin's mother died giving birth to her. Each year, her father, Nozias, feels the wrenching need to earn more money than the small Haitian fishing town of poor Ville Rose can provide and to find someone to care for Claire. Gaelle Lavaud, a fabric shop owner, is a possible mother for the orphaned child, but she is haunted by her own tragic losses. Bernard, who longs to be a journalist and create a radio show that reflects the gang violence of his neighborhood, is caught in the violence himself. Max Junior returns from Miami on a surreptitious mission to visit the girl he impregnated and left years ago and to remember an unrequited love. Louise George, the raspy voice behind a gossipy radio program, is having an affair with Max Senior, head of the local school, and teaches the ethereally beautiful Claire. Their stories and their lives flow one into another.

What secrets have shaped your life?

DATE STARTED:

DATE FINISHED:

MY RATING:

☆ ☆ ☆ ☆ ☆

Evicted: Poverty and Profit in the American City

MATTHEW DESMOND

Andrew Carnegie Medal for Excellence in Nonfiction, 2017 Winner

It is difficult to paint a slumlord as an even remotely sympathetic character, but Harvard professor Matthew Desmond manages to do so in this compelling look at home evictions in Milwaukee, Wisconsin, one of America's most segregated cities. Two landlords are profiled here: Sherrena, who owns dozens of dilapidated units on Milwaukee's infamous North Side, and Tobin, who runs a trailer park on the South Side. They are in it to make money, to be sure, but they also have a tendency to rent to those in need and to look the other way. More often than not, however, they find themselves hauling tenants to eviction court, and here we meet eight families. Among them are Arleen, a single mother dragging her two youngest sons across town in urgent search of a warm, safe place; Scott, a drug addict desperate to crawl up from rock bottom; and Larraine, who loses all of her belongings when she's evicted.

What have you done that was difficult but necessary?

52 Award-Winning Titles Every Book Lover Should Read

This Is How You Lose Her

JUNOT DÍAZ

Andrew Carnegie Medal for Excellence in Fiction, 2013 Finalist

Yunior, a Dominican turned New Jerseyan, is convinced he's not a "bad guy." The women in his life would caustically disagree. We see Yunior as a boy new to America and his long-absent father's temper, as a teenager and college student forever infatuated and forever cheating, and as a lonely adult confronted by aggressive racism. We meet Yunior's combative brother Rafa, Magda the coldhearted, Nilda the young man-magnet, and a sexy older woman. These are precarious, unappreciated, precious lives in which intimacy is a lost art, masculinity a parody, and kindness, reason, and hope struggle to survive like seedlings in a war zone.

What would it be like to find yourself in a new culture?

52 Award-Winning Titles Every Book Lover Should Read

All the Light We Cannot See

ANTHONY DOERR

Andrew Carnegie Medal for Excellence in Fiction, 2015 Winner

Marie-Laure is a sightless girl who lived with her father in Paris before the occupation of France during World War II; her father was a master locksmith for the Museum of Natural History. When the Nazi occupation forces them to abandon the city, Marie-Laure's father takes with him the museum's greatest treasure. He and his daughter eventually arrive at his uncle's house in the coastal city of Saint-Malo. Young German soldier Werner, on the opposite side of the conflagration that is destroying Europe, is sent to Saint-Malo to track Resistance activity there, and inevitably, Marie-Laure's and Werner's paths cross.

If you had to abandon your city, what would you take with you?

DATE STARTED:

DATE FINISHED:

MY RATING:

☆ ☆ ☆ ☆ ☆

52 Award-Winning Titles Every Book Lover Should Read

Manhattan Beach

JENNIFER EGAN

Andrew Carnegie Medal for Excellence in Fiction, 2018 Winner

In 1934, eleven-year-old Anna Kerrigan accompanies her father, Eddie, a union bagman, on a trip to the seaside home of mobster Dexter Styles. Dexter, a dashing and ruthless nightclub impresario, is impressed with Anna's urge to walk barefoot in the frigid sand and sea. "Well, what's it feel like?" he asks. "It only hurts at first," she says. "After a while you can't feel anything." Her father is not pleased, but Dexter grins and says, "Words to live by." Ten years later, her father is gone, and Anna joins the war effort, securing a job at the Brooklyn Naval Yard inspecting parts for battleships. She has an epiphany while watching a man don a massive diving suit: she is destined to be a diver. Her wildly unconventional conviction carries her over every obstacle placed in her way. She also reconnects with Dexter Styles and attempts to discover the fate of her father. Anna does what she believes she must in her search for answers, hope, and ascension.

What did you dream of doing as a child?

_____

_____

_____

Short Nights of the Shadow Catcher: The Epic Life and Immortal Photographs of Edward Curtis

TIMOTHY EGAN

Andrew Carnegie Medal for Excellence in Nonfiction, 2013 Winner

Before half of its twenty volumes were published, *The North American Indian* was called the most important book since the King James Bible. When the last volume emerged, its director and primary researcher and author, self-made master photographer Edward Curtis (1868–1952), was old, broke, and dependent on his daughters. Though his great work consumed $2.5 million of J. P. Morgan's money over the course of three decades, Curtis never took a cent in salary. He lost his business, his property, his marriage, and any control of his great project. But he completed it, preserving a great deal of what we know about Indian cultures, including more than seventy-five languages, thousands of songs and stories, traditional practices in everything from clothing to religious ritual, and the Indian accounts of such historic milestones as the Battle of the Little Bighorn. To accomplish this, he braved the remote, nearly inaccessible places where small tribes clung to their identities, painstakingly won the confidence of wary elders in many larger tribes, and wooed the titans of American wealth to keep going. Curtis's story is frequently suspenseful, always gripping, and monumentally heroic.

What is a challenge you would like to undertake?

DATE STARTED:

DATE FINISHED:

MY RATING:

☆ ☆ ☆ ☆ ☆

The Doomsday Machine: Confessions of a Nuclear War Planner

DANIEL ELLSBERG

Andrew Carnegie Medal for Excellence in Nonfiction, 2018 Finalist

In this gripping and unnerving book of "confessions," author Daniel Ellsberg reveals that along with the top-secret materials about the Vietnam War he copied as a high-clearance strategic analyst at the RAND Corporation and the Defense Department, he also amassed a large cache of classified papers documenting the appalling truth about the perilously inadequate control of nuclear weapons. Ellsberg would have brought these records forward decades ago, but after his trial, which led not to his conviction but to Nixon's resignation, they were lost in a hurricane. Now, thanks to government declassification and online archives, he is finally able to recount with searing specificity such hidden horrors as the delegation of the authority to initiate nuclear attacks, the erroneous assumptions behind the arms race, his role in the Cuban Missile Crisis, and the facts about other near disasters. Entwining affecting personal revelations with jolting governmental disclosures, declaring that Stanley Kubrick's infamous nuclear-weapons satire, *Dr. Strangelove* (1964), "was, essentially, a documentary," and citing our tense standoff with North Korea, Ellsberg concludes his dramatic elucidation of how the nuclear arsenal endangers all of life on Earth with steps for dismantling this Doomsday Machine.

What are the most valuable documents you possess?

The Forgotten Waltz

ANNE ENRIGHT

Andrew Carnegie Medal for Excellence in Fiction, 2012 Winner

Gina Moynihan is married, holds a professional business position, and is now recalling an obsessive, selfish, and problem-riddled affair with the equally married Sean Vallely. Gina remembers that affair not in chronological order but in fits and starts only, eventually concluding at the end. Here is a story of the vicissitudes, obstructions, and collateral damage of an adulterous affair in a milieu rife with mixed feelings and muddled dreams.

Describe your most intense emotional experience.

The Round House

LOUISE ERDRICH

Andrew Carnegie Medal for Excellence in Fiction, 2013 Finalist

Thirteen-year-old Joe Coutts is the son of a tribal judge, Bazil, and a tribal enrollment specialist, Geraldine. He is an attentively loved and lucky boy—until his mother is brutally beaten and raped. Joe and his father try to help Geraldine heal and figure out who attacked her and why. Through Joe's hilarious and unnerving encounters with his ex-stripper aunt, bawdy grandmothers, and a marine turned Catholic priest; Joe's dangerous escapades with his loyal friends; and the spellbinding stories told by his grandfather, Mooshum, Joe awakens to the complexities and traumas of adult life in a poor, racially divisive, yet culturally rich world.

Who are the storytellers in your family, and what are their stories?

Canada

RICHARD FORD

Andrew Carnegie Medal for Excellence in Fiction, 2013 Winner

After fifteen-year-old Dell Parsons's parents rob a bank and are arrested, the trajectory of his life is forever altered. He and his twin sister, Berner, are left to forge their own futures while still reeling from the shock of their parents' desperate act. Berner, burning with resentment, takes off for the West Coast, while a family friend makes arrangements for Dell to hide in Canada. But what Dell discovers in Canada, while in the employ of a mysterious Harvard-educated American with a violent streak, is to take nothing for granted, for "every pillar of the belief the world rests on may or may not be about to explode." Dell not only survives his traumatic adolescence but manages to thrive, while Berner, seemingly more worldly, succumbs to drink and a fractured existence.

What family decision has shifted the trajectory of your life?

52 Award-Winning Titles Every Book Lover Should Read

Fathoms: The World in the Whale

REBECCA GIGGS

Andrew Carnegie Medal for Excellence in Nonfiction, 2021 Winner

Fathoms evokes depth both as a unit of measurement for bodies of water and as "an attempt to understand," writes author Rebecca Giggs. She then takes sea soundings by focusing on the history and current plight of whales, beginning with a beached humpback whale on her home ground in Perth, Australia. Giggs punctuates this encompassing cetacean chronicle with lists of human-generated objects found in dead whales' digestive systems. Even more alarming is how saturated whales are with toxic chemicals: "Inside the whale, the world." With fresh perceptions and cascades of facts, Giggs considers our ancient and persistent whale wonderment, high-tech whale hunting, the 1970s Save the Whales movement, global warming, mass extinction, and pollution, including the oceanic plastic plague. She offers a startling assessment of how smartphones pose new perils for the wild and ponders the loss to our inner lives if we destroy the mystery of the sea. Giggs urges us to save the whales once again, and the oceans, and ourselves.

What do wild places and wild creatures mean to you?

52 Award-Winning Titles Every Book Lover Should Read

Feast Your Eyes

MYLA GOLDBERG

Andrew Carnegie Medal for Excellence in Fiction, 2020 Finalist

Photographer Lillian Preston, chronically shy yet determined, flees Cleveland for New York in 1953 at seventeen and becomes an accidental single mother at nineteen. She loves her daughter, Samantha, but photography rules their threadbare lives. A masterful street photographer, Lillian also passionately photographs her young daughter, who loves posing for her. When she exhibits in a small Brooklyn gallery a series of innocently made photographs of partially clad Samantha, both Lillian and the gallery owner are arrested. This mesmerizing mosaic of a novel takes the form of an unconventional museum-exhibition catalog containing letters, Lillian's journal, and Samantha's piercing commentary on the photographs and her interviews with her mother's few friends. This is a novel of mothers and daughters, art and pain, and transcendent love.

Describe a photo that is important to you.

DATE STARTED:

DATE FINISHED:

MY RATING:

☆ ☆ ☆ ☆ ☆

52 Award-Winning Titles Every Book Lover Should Read

The Bully Pulpit: Theodore Roosevelt, William Howard Taft, and the Golden Age of Journalism

DORIS KEARNS GOODWIN

Andrew Carnegie Medal for Excellence in Nonfiction, 2014 Winner

In the Progressive movement of the early twentieth century, an activist federal government that promoted both social and economic progress crossed party lines. Goodwin, the acclaimed historian, repeatedly emphasizes that fact in her massive and masterful study of the friendship, and then the enmity, of two presidents who played major roles in that movement. Roosevelt, unsurprisingly, is portrayed as egotistical, bombastic, and determined to take on powerful special interests. He saw his secretary of war, Taft, as a friend and disciple. When Taft, as president, seemed to abandon the path of reform, Roosevelt saw it as both a political and a personal betrayal. Taft receives nuanced, sympathetic, but not particularly favorable treatment here. Also examined are some of the great journalists who exposed societal ills and promoted the reforms that aimed to address them, including Ida Tarbell and Lincoln Steffens of *McClure's Magazine*. This book re-creates a period when many politicians, journalists, and citizens of differing political affiliations viewed government as a force for public good.

Who was your favorite president, and why?

DATE STARTED:

DATE FINISHED:

MY RATING:

☆ ☆ ☆ ☆ ☆

52 Award-Winning Titles Every Book Lover Should Read

Killers of the Flower Moon: The Osage Murders and the Birth of the FBI

DAVID GRANN

Andrew Carnegie Medal for Excellence in Nonfiction, 2018 Finalist

During the early 1920s, many members of the Osage Indian Nation were murdered, one by one. After being forced from several home-lands, the Osage had settled in the late nineteenth century in an unoccupied area of Oklahoma, chosen precisely because it was "rocky, sterile, and utterly unfit for cultivation." No white man would covet this land; Osage people would be happy. Then oil was soon discovered below the Osage territory, speedily attracting prospec-tors wielding staggering sums and turning many Osage into some of the richest people in the world. This true-crime mystery centers on Mollie Burkhart, an Osage woman who lost several family members as the death tally grew, and Tom White, the former Texas Ranger whom J. Edgar Hoover sent to solve the slippery, attention-grabbing case once and for all.

What mystery in your life (or in your family history) would you like to resolve?

Midnight in Chernobyl: The Untold Story of the World's Greatest Nuclear Disaster

ADAM HIGGINBOTHAM

Andrew Carnegie Medal for Excellence in Nonfiction, 2020 Winner

Midnight in Chernobyl is a top-notch historical narrative: a tense, fast-paced, engrossing, and revelatory product of more than a decade of research. Author Adam Higginbotham interviewed most of the surviving central participants in the disaster, examined volumes of newly declassified Soviet documents, and surveyed previous research and reportage. The result is a stunningly detailed account of the explosion of Reactor Four at the Chernobyl nuclear power plant on April 26, 1986. It offers a brief history of the development of the Soviet nuclear power program leading up to the construction of the plant at Chernobyl, a second-by-second account of the night of the accident, the confluence of causes, the evacuation of the surrounding countryside, the containment and cleanup efforts, and a deep dive into the aftermath: the medical and environmental consequences, the political machinations and missteps, the role Chernobyl played in the downfall of the USSR, and the effect it had on the pursuit of nuclear power worldwide. Higginbotham humanizes the tale, maintaining a focus on the people involved and the choices they made, both heroic and not, in unimaginable circumstances.

Describe a heroic action you took to help others.

DATE STARTED:

DATE FINISHED:

MY RATING:

☆ ☆ ☆ ☆ ☆

52 Award-Winning Titles Every Book Lover Should Read

Hello, Universe

ERIN ENTRADA KELLY

John Newbery Medal, 2018 Winner

Four middle schoolers' fates intertwine one summer. Scrawny, taciturn Virgil Salinas can generally be found caring for his guinea pig and avoiding neighborhood bully Chet Bullens. The only people he feels comfortable around are his *lola* (his Filipino grandmother) and his Japanese American friend Kaori, who fancies herself a psychic. Kaori's quirky self-confidence is a foil to Virgil's insecurities, and when he comes to her for help befriending a girl in his class, Valencia Somerset, she can't wait to consult her star chart. For her own part, Valencia struggles with nightmares after being rejected by her best friend, and the fact that she's deaf hasn't made finding new friends easy. When she spots Kaori's "business card" on a notice board, she makes an appointment to discuss her troubling dreams. That very day, Virgil goes missing, and Valencia joins Kaori's search for the boy. Rather than holding her back, Valencia's deafness heightens her perceptiveness.

How do your and your friends' lives intertwine?

----

52 Award-Winning Titles Every Book Lover Should Read

Dig

A. S. KING

Michael L. Printz Award for Excellence in Young Adult Literature, 2020 Winner

Five unknowingly connected teens grapple with their identities within the context of their families and society. Trauma or abuse touches most of their lives, and they each find security in a self-defined role. The Shoveler's snow shovel may give him a reputation for being strange, but it also keeps him safe from school bullies. The Freak flickers from location to location, always in control of her ability to exit a situation. Malcolm's frequent first-class flights to Jamaica give a charmed veneer to a life otherwise dictated by his father's cancer. Loretta is ringmistress of a flea circus and knows her part by heart, even when her father goes dangerously off script. CanIHelpYou? works the Arby's drive-through, discreetly serving drugs to those who know the magic words. These characters brush against one another's lives, eventually coming together at an eye-opening Easter dinner.

Give yourself nicknames for the roles you play in your life.

The Crossover

KWAME ALEXANDER

John Newbery Medal, 2015 Winner

The Bell twins are stars on the basketball court and comrades in life. While there are some differences—Josh shaves his head and Jordan loves his locks—both twins adhere to the Bell basketball rules: "In this game of life, your family is the court, and the ball is your heart." With a former professional basketball player dad and an assistant principal mom, there is an intensely strong home front supporting sports and education in equal measures. When life intervenes in the form of a hot new girl, the balance shifts and growing apart proves painful.

How have your evolving interests changed your relation-ships?

52 Award-Winning Titles Every Book Lover Should Read

We Are Okay

NINA LACOUR

*Michael L. Printz Award for Excellence in
Young Adult Literature, 2018 Winner*

It's the winter break during Marin's first year at college, and she is facing the holidays thousands of miles from her San Francisco home. Since her grandfather died the previous summer, Marin feels set adrift. Not only has she lost Gramps, her sole caretaker, but he'd been keeping secrets, and when she discovers the truth, it shatters everything she believed about her life. Engulfed in pain and feeling alone, she shuns her best friend Mabel's numerous calls and texts. But Mabel flies cross-country, determined to help her friend deal with her grief. Marin is afraid that Mabel regrets the physical intimacy that had grown between the two girls while she was still in California and braces herself for more heartache, but Mabel surprises her in more ways than one.

Describe a time when you traveled to comfort a friend.

Heavy: An American Memoir

KIESE LAYMON

Andrew Carnegie Medal for Excellence in Nonfiction, 2019 Winner

In his spectacular memoir, author Kiese Laymon recalls the traumas of his Mississippi youth. He captures his confusion at being molested by his babysitter and at witnessing older boys abuse a girl he liked; at having no food in the house despite his mother's brilliance; at being beaten and loved ferociously, often at the same time. His hungry mind and body grow until, like flipping a switch, at college he is compelled to shrink himself with a punishing combination of diet and exercise. Laymon applies his book's title to his body and his memories, to his inheritance as a student, a teacher, a writer, an activist, a Black man, and his mother's son—but also to the weight of truth, and writing it.

What feels "heavy" in your life right now? How does writing uplift you?

DATE STARTED:

DATE FINISHED:

MY RATING:

☆ ☆ ☆ ☆ ☆

52 Award-Winning Titles Every Book Lover Should Read

28

On Such a Full Sea

CHANG-RAE LEE

Andrew Carnegie Medal for Excellence in Fiction, 2015 Finalist

B-Mor is a rigorously ordered labor settlement founded in what used to be Baltimore by refugees from impossibly polluted New China. They grow stringently regulated food for the elite, who live in gated "charter" villages, surrounded by "open counties," in which civilization has collapsed under the assaults of a pandemic and an ever-harsher climate. Young, small, yet mighty Fan, a breath-held diver, is preternaturally at home among the farmed fish she tends to. When her boyfriend inexplicably disappears, Fan escapes from B-Mor to search for him. She encounters a taciturn healer bereft of all that he cherished, a troupe of backwoods acrobats, and a disturbing cloister of girls creating an intricate mural of their muffled lives on her daring quest in a violent, blighted world.

Where do you feel most at home?

52 Award-Winning Titles Every Book Lover Should Read

29

March: Book Three

JOHN LEWIS AND ANDREW AYDIN,
ILLUSTRATED BY NATE POWELL

*Michael L. Printz Award for Excellence in
Young Adult Literature, 2017 Winner*

Opening with the bombing of the Birmingham Baptist Church, *March: Book Three* highlights the growing violence and tensions among activists in the civil rights movement leading up to Freedom Summer and President Johnson's eventual signing of the Voting Rights Act of 1965. As protests and marches—and sometimes merely being Black—in Alabama became increasingly dangerous, opinions among activists in the movement were divided. Continue to march and risk serious harm? Or put their trust in white leaders who were only willing to meet them partway? The message in this book is abundantly clear: the victories of the civil rights movement are hard-won and only succeed through the dogged dedication of a wide variety of people.

How are you engaged in your community?

DATE STARTED:

DATE FINISHED:

MY RATING:

☆ ☆ ☆ ☆ ☆

52 Award-Winning Titles Every Book Lover Should Read

Lost Children Archive

VALERIA LUISELLI

Andrew Carnegie Medal for Excellence in Fiction, 2020 Winner

An unnamed couple and their children embark on a cross-country road trip from New York City to Arizona. Husband and wife both work as audio recording artists, dedicated to capturing the soundscapes of everyday life. Upon their arrival, he plans to investigate the native Apache people who used to populate the Southwest, and she has promised to find a friend's daughters who have been arrested at the border. When the family arrives at their destination, however, the overwhelming scale of the migrant crisis redirects their efforts, and the children eventually lose themselves in the strange, uncertain terrain. Husband and wife rush to recover their own offspring in this unsettling situation.

Describe a time in your life when you felt lost.

52 Award-Winning Titles Every Book Lover Should Read

Dopesick: Dealers, Doctors, and the Drug Company That Addicted America

BETH MACY

Andrew Carnegie Medal for Excellence in Nonfiction, 2019 Finalist

"Dopesick," street lingo for narcotics withdrawal, is also used metaphorically here for addictive opioids' damage of families, neighborhoods, and the nation itself. Award-winning journalist Beth Macy details America's opioid addiction, starting with one dealer's arrival in a small Virginia town (Appalachia is most impacted by this national-health menace), which results in high school football players being included in the growing numbers of heroin-overdose fatalities. She captures the wretched voices of grieving parents questioning why their boys died and the broken words of neighbors, shattered as drug abuses and deaths of their depressed, unemployed husbands multiply, the result of painkiller overuse. Tracking the progression of addiction from 1996, with OxyContin typically overprescribed for injury and postsurgical pain, Macy leads readers through the inevitable and dreadful downward spiral of addiction. Still, Macy suggests that there may be hope.

How does hope inspire change?

52 Award-Winning Titles Every Book Lover Should Read

The Great Believers

REBECCA MAKKAI

Andrew Carnegie Medal for Excellence in Fiction, 2019 Winner

It is 1985, and Yale has just lost his friend Nico to AIDS. This is not the first time, nor nearly the last, that he'll lose a loved one to the terrifying, still-mysterious disease. Soon after, Nico's younger sister and Yale's friend Fiona connects Yale to her nonagenarian great-aunt, who studied art in Paris in the 1910s and now wants to donate her personal collection of never-before-seen work by now-famous artists to the Northwestern University art gallery, where Yale works in development. This potentially career-making discovery arrives along with a crushing reveal in Yale's personal life. Another thread throughout the novel begins in 2015 as Fiona flies to Paris, where she has reason to believe her long-estranged adult daughter now lives. Yale and Fiona wrestle with painful pasts and fight to find joy in the present.

Write about your "chosen family."

Hold Still: A Memoir with Photographs

SALLY MANN

Andrew Carnegie Medal for Excellence in Nonfiction, 2016 Winner

Writing was photographer Sally Mann's first creative calling, and her prose has the same firepower as the many photographs that illustrate this searching, witty, and gothic inquiry into family, place, and art. Mann confesses her aversion to wearing clothes as a "near-feral child" and her lifelong love for the land on which she and her husband have lived for more than forty years. She also shares, for the first time, the dark side of her notoriety, as well as the daring adventures behind more recent photographic series. Here, too, are staggering family secrets, including her in-laws' deceptive lives and violent deaths, her Mayflower-blue-blood mother's scandalously unconventional childhood, and her self-sacrificing, country-doctor father's complicated legacy of slave ownership, wealth, and philanthropy. Mann also scrutinizes her relationship with Gee-Gee, the African American woman who ran their household for fifty years. *Hold Still* is a boldly alive, bracingly honest, thoroughly engrossing, sun-dappled, and deeply shadowed tale of inheritance and defiance, creativity and remembrance by an audacious and tenacious American photographer.

52 Award-Winning Titles Every Book Lover Should Read

What are your favorite family photographs?

DATE STARTED:

DATE FINISHED:

MY RATING:

☆ ☆ ☆ ☆ ☆

52 Award-Winning Titles Every Book Lover Should Read

Catherine the Great: Portrait of a Woman

ROBERT K. MASSIE

Andrew Carnegie Medal for Excellence in Nonfiction, 2012 Winner

Sophie of Anhalt-Zerbst, as Catherine the Great was originally named, appeals to readers for several reasons. Those interested in the expansion and development of the Russian Empire under her reign (1762–96) can delve into her conduct of war and diplomacy, cultivation of Enlightenment notables, and attempted reforms of law and government. And those fascinated by the intimate intrigues of dynasties will find an extraordinary example in Catherine's ascent from minor German princess to absolute autocrat of Russia. Included is Catherine's own account of surviving palace politics as consort to the eccentric and disliked crown prince, Paul, and allusions to her liaisons with courtiers, most famously, Grigory Potemkin. Massie humanizes the real woman behind the imperial persona.

Who are your favorite royals, and why?

Last Stop on Market Street

MATT DE LA PEÑA, ILLUSTRATED
BY CHRISTIAN ROBINSON

John Newbery Medal, 2016 Winner

CJ and his nana depart church and make it to the bus stop just in time to avoid an oncoming rain shower. They board the bus, and while CJ is full of questions and complaints (Why don't they have a car? Why must they make this trip every week? and so forth), Nana's resolute responses articulate the glories of their rich, vibrant life in the city as presented by the bus's passengers and passages. A tattooed man checks his cell phone. An older woman keeps butterflies in a jar. A musician tunes and plays his guitar. At last the pair arrive at Market Street and proceed to the soup kitchen where, upon recognizing friendly faces, CJ is glad they came to help. This children's picture book reflects a picture of a community that resonates with harmony and diversity.

In what unexpected places have you found beauty?

52 Award-Winning Titles Every Book Lover Should Read

Merci Suárez Changes Gears

MEG MEDINA

John Newbery Medal, 2019 Winner

Merci Suárez loves painting with her papi, playing on his soccer team, telling her abuelo Lolo about her days at school, and taking pictures of her family when they are together. But lately Lolo has been acting different—he wanders off, forgets things easily, and has even gotten angry. To add to Merci's worries, sixth grade at Seaward Pines Academy has gotten off to a rocky start. To make up her school tuition, Merci has been assigned community service as a Sunshine Buddy to new student Michael Clark, and as the weeks go by, popular Edna Santos only gets meaner as Merci and Michael become friends. Merci isn't sure what to make of this new world where "maybe like" is not the same as "like like" and where "popular" is not the same as having friends. As she navigates her way through the year, she discovers that even though change is scary and even though it may mean things will never be the same, sometimes it is unavoidable.

What changes in your life have brought you greater happiness?

DATE STARTED:

DATE FINISHED:

MY RATING:

☆ ☆ ☆ ☆ ☆

I'll Give You the Sun

JANDY NELSON

Michael L. Printz Award for Excellence in
Young Adult Literature, 2015 Winner

When Noah's mom suggests that he and his twin sister, Jude, apply to a prestigious art high school, he is elated, but Jude starts simmering with jealousy when it becomes clear that their mother favors Noah's work. Noah soaks up the praise, though a little callously, happy to hone his painting skills and focus on the guy across the street, who could be more than a friend. Fast-forward three years, and everything is in pieces. Their mother has died in a car crash, and Noah, who wasn't accepted into the art school, has given up painting, while Jude, who was accepted but is no longer the shimmering, confident girl she once was, is struggling in her sculpture class. All her clay forms shatter in the kiln; is her mother's ghost the culprit? Determined to make a piece that her mother can't ruin, Jude seeks out the mentorship of a fiery stone carver and his alluring model, Oscar.

What art form moves you, and how?

52 Award-Winning Titles Every Book Lover Should Read

The Sympathizer

VIET THANH NGUYEN

Andrew Carnegie Medal for Excellence in Fiction, 2016 Winner

Adept in the merciless art of interrogation, the nameless spy who narrates this dark novel knows how to pry answers from the unwilling. Unexpectedly, however, this Vietnamese Communist sympathizer finds himself being tortured by the very revolutionary zealots he has helped make victorious in Saigon. He responds to this torture by extending an intense self-interrogation already underway before his incarceration. The narrator thus plumbs his singular double-mindedness by reliving his turbulent life as the bastard son of a French priest and a devout Asian mother. Haunted by a faith he no longer accepts, insecure in the Communist ideology he has embraced, the spy sweeps a vision sharpened by disillusionment across the tangled individual psyches of those close to him—a friend, a lover, a comrade—and into the warped motives of the imperialists and ideologues governing the world he must navigate.

How have your beliefs evolved over time?

There There

TOMMY ORANGE

Andrew Carnegie Medal for Excellence in Fiction, 2019 Finalist

The upcoming Big Oakland Powwow brings together many at-first disconnected individuals. Some have been working on the event for months, some will sneak in with only good intentions, while others are plotting to steal the sizable cash prizes. Opal recalls occupying Alcatraz as a child with her family; today, she raises her sister's grandchildren as her own after their unspeakable loss. With grant support, Dene endeavors to complete the oral-history project his deceased uncle couldn't, recording the stories of Indians living in Oakland. In his thirties, with his white mother's blessing, Edwin reaches out to the Native father he never met. Each of them wrestles with what it means to be Native American.

What are the most inspiring parts of your grandparents' life stories?

52 Award-Winning Titles Every Book Lover Should Read

Blood at the Root: A Racial Cleansing in America

PATRICK PHILLIPS

Andrew Carnegie Medal for Excellence in Nonfiction, 2017 Finalist

From murder to rape to robbery, virtually every crime committed in the rural Atlanta farming community of Forsyth County, Georgia, in 1912 was attributed to marauding Black men. The fact that there was no credible evidence to support these beliefs was secondary; white townspeople rushed to judgment, assigning guilt and sentencing to death the Black men they deemed responsible. Lynchings were commonplace. Night-riding arsonists burned and bombed Black families out of their homes, turning Forsyth County into a whites-only enclave, segregation that would endure for decades. Author Patrick Phillips, the child of parents who were part of a small cadre of white homeowners brave enough to challenge the status quo, tells the story of ethnic profiling and its elaborate cover-up in this disquieting account of an underreported chapter in America's racial history.

Describe a time when someone stood up for you.

Figuring

MARIA POPOVA

Andrew Carnegie Medal for Excellence in Nonfiction, 2020 Finalist

Maria Popova, the ever-curious thinker behind the celebrated website Brain Pickings, brings her hunger for facts and zeal for biography to this mind-opening, category-defying study of the mysteriously intertwining forces of science, literature, art, and interpersonal love that have driven some of humanity's most illuminating discoveries. The revelation here is how few degrees separate key figures, from Herman Melville to Emily Dickinson to Rachel Carson. Melville looks through Maria Mitchell's telescope as artist Harriet Hosmer associates with Melville's beloved Nathaniel Hawthorne in Rome while sculpting the enfolded hands of Robert and Elizabeth Barrett Browning, whose work inspired Dickinson, and on and on.

What are you most curious about currently?

52 Award-Winning Titles Every Book Lover Should Read

Spillover: Animal Infections and the Next Human Pandemic

DAVID QUAMMEN

Andrew Carnegie Medal for Excellence in Nonfiction, 2013 Finalist

Science writer David Quammen schools us in the fascinating if alarming facts about zoonotic diseases—animal infections that sicken humans, such as rabies, Ebola, influenza, and West Nile. Zoonoses can escalate rapidly into global pandemics when "human-to-human transmission" occurs, and Quammen wants us to understand disease dynamics and exactly what's at stake. Drawing on the truly dramatic history of virology, he profiles brave and stubborn viral sleuths and recounts his own hair-raising field adventures, including helping capture large fruit bats in Bangladesh. Along the way, Quammen explains how devilishly difficult it is to trace the origins of a zoonosis and explicates the hidden process by which pathogens "spill over" from their respective reservoir hosts (water fowl, mosquitoes, pigs, bats, monkeys) and infect humans.

What field of science or discovery most intrigues you, and why?

52 Award-Winning Titles Every Book Lover Should Read

Bone Gap

LAURA RUBY

*Michael L. Printz Award for Excellence in
Young Adult Literature, 2016 Winner*

For all appearances, Bone Gap is a sluggish farming town that most people want to escape, a place "with gaps just wide enough for people to slip away...leaving only their stories behind." That's what folks assume happened when Roza disappeared from the state fair, but seventeen-year-old Finn knows better. He's the only one who sees her leave, but his description of her abductor—that he moves like a shivering cornstalk—doesn't help the police, and the people of Bone Gap resentfully believe that Finn helped the beloved girl disappear because she wanted to. Her departure drives a wedge between Finn and his brother Sean—Finn feels like Sean isn't doing enough to look for her, and Sean thinks Finn is hiding something about the night she left. The gaps in Bone are "gaps in the world. In the space of things." Those gaps in the town are loose enough that a person can fall clear through to the other side of reality, and that's precisely where the cornstalk man took Roza and where Finn must go to rescue her.

How are your powers of observation? What do you see that other people miss?

52 Award-Winning Titles Every Book Lover Should Read

Swamplandia!

KAREN RUSSELL

Andrew Carnegie Medal for Excellence in Fiction, 2012 Finalist

Swamplandia! is a shabby tourist attraction deep in the Everglades, owned by the Bigtree clan of alligator wrestlers. When Hilola, their star performer, dies, her husband and children lose their moorings, and Swamplandia! itself is endangered as audiences dwindle. The Chief leaves. Brother Kiwi, seventeen, sneaks off to work at the World of Darkness, a new mainland amusement park featuring the "rings of hell." Otherworldly sister Osceola, sixteen, vanishes after falling in love with the ghost of a young man who died while working for the ill-fated Dredge and Fill Campaign in the 1930s. It is up to Ava, thirteen, to find her sister, and her odyssey to the Underworld is mythic, spellbinding, and terrifying.

Fantasize a perfect vacation destination.

52 Award-Winning Titles Every Book Lover Should Read

Lincoln in the Bardo

GEORGE SAUNDERS

Andrew Carnegie Medal for Excellence in Fiction, 2018 Finalist

Anchored to a historical moment—the death of President Abraham Lincoln's young son, Willie, in February 1862—the surreal action in this story takes place in a cemetery, when Lincoln enters the crypt to hold his boy's body one last time. Scenes of epic sorrow turn grotesque as a choir of specters caught in the bardo—the mysterious transitional state following death and preceding rebirth, heaven, or hell—tell their stories, which range from the gleefully ribald to the tragic in tales embodying the dire conflicts underlying the then-raging Civil War in this macabre carnival of the dead.

What historical moment most intrigues you?

52 Award-Winning Titles Every Book Lover Should Read

The Book of Aron

JIM SHEPARD

Andrew Carnegie Medal for Excellence in Fiction, 2016 Finalist

Aron is a hopelessly inept Jewish village boy who despairs over his inability to learn the most basic things. Yet he discovers hidden strengths and talents when his family moves to Warsaw and the Nazis erect the walls that formed the Jewish ghetto, hell on earth for hundreds of thousands of brutally confined, starving people. Newly enterprising and courageous Aron helps his family by scrounging, stealing, lying, and smuggling as corruption and coercion become the order of the day. With other brave, crafty, and hungry children, he forms a band of intrepid looters, only to become entangled with a treacherously venal policeman. As life grows impossibly danger-ous and terrifying and families are taken away to be gassed, Aron finds refuge with the real-life Warsaw Ghetto hero Janusz Korczak, a Jewish pediatrician and children's advocate who founded an orphanage and refused to abandon those in his care.

What are your hidden strengths and talents?

Swing Time

ZADIE SMITH

Andrew Carnegie Medal for Excellence in Fiction, 2017 Finalist

The unnamed narrator in this story is entranced and provoked by a Fred Astaire dance number in the movie *Swing Time*. Though passionate and knowledgeable about dance, especially pioneering African American tap stars Jeni LeGon and the Nicholas Brothers, the narrator doesn't have the body for it, while her childhood best friend, Tracey, has the requisite build and drive. Both "brown girls" lived in a London housing project in the early 1980s—the narrator with her ambitiously political Jamaican mother and her laid-back white father, Tracey with her white mother while longing for her Black father whose appearances were infrequent and fraught. Close as they are, the girls are destined for diverging paths as Tracey stakes her future on dance and the narrator muddles through a goth phase and college, then lucks into a job as a personal assistant to an international pop star, the fiercely willful, strikingly pale Aimee, who hijacks her life.

What art form inspires you the most?

Just Mercy: A Story of Justice and Redemption

BRYAN STEVENSON

Andrew Carnegie Medal for Excellence in Nonfiction, 2015 Winner

As a young Harvard law student testing himself in an internship in Georgia, author Bryan Stevenson visited death-row inmates and saw firsthand the injustices suffered by the poor and disadvantaged, how too many had been railroaded into convictions with inadequate legal representation. The visit made such an impression on Stevenson that he started the Equal Justice Institute in Montgomery, Alabama. One of his first clients was Walter McMillian, a young Black man accused of murdering a white woman and imprisoned on death row even before he was tried. Stevenson alternates chapters on the shocking miscarriage of justice in McMillian's case, including police and prosecutorial misconduct, with other startling cases. Among the cases Stevenson cites are a fourteen-year-old condemned to death for killing his mother's abusive boyfriend and a mentally ill adolescent girl condemned to life in prison for second-degree murder for the death of young boys killed in a fire she started accidentally. Through these cases and others, Stevenson details changes in victims' rights, incarceration of juveniles, death penalty reforms, inflexible sentencing laws, and the continued practices of injustice that see too many juveniles, minorities, and mentally ill people imprisoned in a frenzy of mass incarceration in the United States.

When and how have you been inspired to work on improving the lives of others?

DATE STARTED:

DATE FINISHED:

MY RATING:

☆ ☆ ☆ ☆ ☆

52 Award-Winning Titles Every Book Lover Should Read

The Goldfinch

DONNA TARTT

Andrew Carnegie Medal for Excellence in Fiction, 2014 Winner

In the wake of his nefarious father's abandonment, Theo, a smart thirteen-year-old Manhattanite, is extremely close to his vivacious mother—until an act of terrorism catapults him into a dizzying world bereft of gravity, certainty, or love. Theo first seeks sanctuary with a troubled Park Avenue family and, in Greenwich Village, with a kind and gifted restorer of antique furniture. Fate then delivers Theo to utterly alien Las Vegas, where he meets young outlaw Boris. As Theo, stricken with grief and post-traumatic stress disorder, becomes a complexly damaged adult, he is pulled into the shadowlands of art, lashed to seventeenth-century Dutch artist Carel Fabritius and his exquisite if sinister painting *The Goldfinch*.

Is there a piece of art you are connected to or moved by?

Nora Webster

COLM TÓIBÍN

Andrew Carnegie Medal for Excellence in Fiction, 2015 Finalist

With the early death of her beloved Maurice, fortysomething Nora Webster becomes a widow with four children and scarcely enough money to cover the family expenses. Nora must step out of the rather cocoon-like world she and her husband had created for themselves in the small city of Wexford, Ireland. "The problem for her was that she was on her own now and that she had no idea how to live." Her sisters, aunts, and friends all offer assistance and advice as she navigates unfamiliar terrain. Can she put the memory of Maurice to the side and create a new life?

Describe a bold, independent, and fierce woman you know.

Sing, Unburied, Sing

JESMYN WARD

Andrew Carnegie Medal for Excellence in Fiction, 2018 Finalist

Jojo, thirteen, and his three-year-old sister, Kayla, live with their grandparents, Mam and Pop, in rural Mississippi, while their mother, Leonie, struggles with drug addiction and her failures as a daughter, mother, and inheritor of a gift (or curse) that connects her to spirits. Leonie insists that Jojo and Kayla accompany her on a two-day journey to the infamous Parchman prison to retrieve their white father. Their harrowing experiences are bound up in unresolved and reverberating racial and family tensions and entanglements: long-buried memories of Pop's time in Parchman, the imminent death of Mam from cancer, and the slow dawning of the children's own spiritual gifts.

What do you consider to be your greatest gift?

Sing, Unburied, Sing

52 Award-Winning Titles Every Book Lover Should Read

The Underground Railroad

COLSON WHITEHEAD

Andrew Carnegie Medal for Excellence in Fiction, 2017 Winner

Smart and resilient Cora, a young third-generation slave on a Georgia cotton plantation, has been brutally attacked by whites and Blacks. Certain that the horror will only get worse, she flees with a young man who knows how to reach the Underground Railroad, an actual railroad running through tunnels dug beneath the blood-soaked fields of the South. Yet freedom proves miserably elusive. A South Carolina town appears to be welcoming until Cora discovers that it is all a facade, concealing quasi-medical genocidal schemes. With a notoriously relentless slave catcher following close behind, Cora endures another terrifying underground journey, arriving in North Carolina, where the corpses of tortured Black people hang on the trees along a road whites call the Freedom Trail. Each stop Cora makes along the Underground Railroad reveals another shocking and malignant symptom of a country riven by catastrophic conflicts, a poisonous moral crisis, and diabolical violence.

Write about an unforgettable journey you've taken.

52 Award-Winning Titles Every Book Lover Should Read

ABOUT THE
AMERICAN LIBRARY
ASSOCIATION

The American Library Association (ALA) is the trusted voice of libraries and the national organization that provides resources to inspire library and information workers to transform their communities through essential programs and services. The association is committed to using a social justice framework in its work, with key areas including advocacy for libraries and for the profession, diversity, education and lifelong learning, equitable access to information and library services for all, intellectual freedom, literacy, sustainability, and the transformation of libraries.

The reviews in this book come from *Booklist*, the book review magazine of the American Library Association and an invaluable source of reading recommendations for all readers. *Booklist* is an essential collection development and readers' advisory tool for thousands of librarians. For more information, visit booklistonline.com.

Learn more about how you can stay connected to what's going on in libraries and how you can help advocate for your own library at ilovelibraries.org.